THE STOCK MARKET IS SIMPLE FOR TEENAGERS AND ADULTS

BEGINNERS LEARN INVESTING WITH LOW RISK

Karen Jean Antoinette D'Alessandro
PRESIDENT & FOUNDER
SAIS Inc.

ISBN: 979-8-218-11531-9

DEDICATION:

FOR THE HOMELESS CATS AND DOGS IN HIGH KILL ANIMAL SHELTERS. OUR CHARITY PULLS THEM FROM THE HIGH KILL ANIMAL SHELTERS TO SAVE THEIR LIVES. ALL PROFITS WILL GO DIRECTLY TO THE THEM.

I AM THE FOUNDER OF SAVE ANIMALS IN SHELTERS, INC. A NOT-FOR-PROFIT CHARITY THAT EDUCATES THE PUBLIC ON ANIMAL WELFARE. WE SELL MANY ITEMS IN WALMART, ETSY ETC. WE GENERATE FUNDS TO BE DONATED TO SAVE THE HOMELESS CATS AND DOGS. THEN WE PLACE THEM IN LOVING HOMES.

TABLE OF CONTENTS

ACKNOWLEDGMENTS

This goes out to my Uncle Teddy. As a kid, I always remember him speaking about the stock market, especially during the holidays. He shared his knowledge early on to me. Until we meet again, I will carry on with my studies.

1. THE STOCK MARKET

Okay, let's get right into it.   Why does the stock market keep going up over time. If you look back in time from 1900 it keeps climbing. Each day, in the world 385,000 babies are born. Each day in the world, 183,000 die.

One of the main reasons is the more people in the world the more money in the stock market.

Why does the market go up and down?   One of the main reasons is people's emotions. Yes, it is not a magical formula from a brilliant genius. Just listen to the News and the public usually responds. People will hear good News and think it is a good time to buy. People will hear the bad News and they will panic and sell. Why does the stock market go up and down?

One of the main reasons is people's emotions.

There are ups and downs but over-all it is up as the years past. You will read the average stock market return is 8 to 10 percent. It will vary because people do receive money along the way. I will explain that later, one step at a time.

Is there a safer more conservative way to buy into the stock market? Yes, there are mutual funds and ETF's (exchange traded funds) Wow, that sounds complicated. No, it is probably a term you have not heard in the past. Just follow me with my simple explanation.

There are funds that mirror the overall stock market performance year after year.

The funds I am writing about are called index funds. We are going to discuss the one index fund that measures the total stock market, S&P. It stands for Standard and Poor's company. It is nationally known and widely used as a data source and issuers for credit ratings.

This is one of the largest credit rating companies in the world. The company dates back around 1860 or close to that time. The American stock market is the largest in the world.

When people mention the stock market, they are referencing the S&P. This is the most popular measure of the stock market in the world.

It is known as the S&P 500. The S&P 500 consists of 500 largest publicly traded companies in the USA. Many are highly familiar names: Apple, Exxon Mobile, Visa, Coca-Cola, Bank of America, and Microsoft.

To qualify for the S&P 500 Index, a company must have at least 10% of its shares outstanding in the public market and have a market capitalization of at least 13.1 billion. There are very few companies that can be a part of those qualifications.

People often talk about how they are successful with their investments. Maybe it is luck which could very well be. Overall, the rule is to **diversify with investments.**

Basically, it means to have your money invested in many different places. It could be cash in a bank, a savings account at work, a pension plan, a house with value, cars, jewelry and much more.

For example, you have money in the bank and you bought this antique car that you heard will go up in value. Perhaps like double for what you bought it for. You think you are set. After three years of owning this car, they find a major default in the engine that cannot be fixed. Your antique car lost its complete value. You are just left with money in the bank.

To diversify will make your financial plan safer. If you have your money in all different places, it will shelter you from loss if one of these investments are not doing well.

We are done. Class is over just shut the book and slip out the back door. Go ahead over to the beach and/or go to the golf course.

Obviously, I need to explain some details to get you started or this book will not be published. Seriously, those are the main key factors in the stock market and personal financial facts. If you just read above and understand you know more than most people. Just ask a few people those questions and you will be surprised.

As a matter of fact, they will ask where did you find out this information? Did you read that information? Well, you can just say whatever you want. Give yourself credit for it. After all you did take the time to read this book.

Reading a book about the stock market is not an easy task to seek. Although, with me you will find an easy solution. I learned by experience, so it will make this book easy to read.

Okay, where was I? Here is a simple chart of the history of the stock market. You will see where it dips and many of them are because there was a major-event. They are rare and that is why they are called the black swan.

If we think of 9-11 and the housing crisis there was a dip in the stock market. What do you think was the worse dip from these 2 events in the stock market? It was the housing market.

CHAPTER 2. LET'S TRADE CARROTS FOR CORN

Is everyone still a wake? Good. To follow is the history of the stock market. By learning the history, it will make more sense, to know today's stock market. Let's take a step back on how and why it started.

Back in the day people traded items because they wanted more goods. If I grew carrots and potatoes and you grew apples and corn, we would trade. It was a good way to obtain more goods.

Money was created, so people can trade goods and services for a price that would be fair market value. For example, if Terry D had a necklace that is 16 inches long and solid 14k gold and Gene D had a necklace that is 16 inches long solid sterling silver there would be a great price difference.

Obviously, people want to know they obtain a fair price that fits their goods and services. Imagine if money was not created. Then clearly there would not be any international trade.

Let's review a few stock market examples. You buy a stock share in the company called Sun and Fun. You pay $10 dollars for one stock share. The company grows and opens more stores. The stock share just went up to $15 dollars. You made a $5 dollar profit with one stock share. That is if you sell that stock share at that time.

However, it can work the opposite. You buy a stock share in the company called Orange and White. You pay $20 dollars for one stock share. The stock share goes down to $15 dollars for one stock share. So, you lost $5 dollars on one stock share. That is if you sell that stock share at that time.

CHAPTER 3 - THE PUBLIC'S REACTION

People react to the stock market in many different ways when it goes up and down. It basically depends on their knowledge of the stock market. Also, how much time you have for your goals. There could be many reasons. People buy into the stock market at all different times so they receive all different prices of stocks and funds

I told my father when he reached 65, sell out of the stock market. The market was high. As we get older, we want to make sure our money is safe. You can easily need your money in a year. If you invest in the stock market I believe, you should have at least 3 to 5 years of time. If you want to make an overnight immediate profit the stock market may not be for you.

Here are some real examples: People will buy stocks if someone or company found the cure to cancer. It is a miracle. For decades there were no major developments. People are elated and realize this is the key to a much longer life.

They will invest money in that particular company stock or funds. Also, they will invest in stocks or funds that are similar.   They will even buy onto a company who may be a part of this revelation. Here is an example, the packaging of this particular drug.

Even if they hear the stock or fund has done great for years, they all want to buy. That's all it takes to get the market to rise. It is truly exciting thinking and hoping to make money.

Unemployment News is another trigger to get the stock market going up or down. There is also at any given time, a country can affect another country.

The public will take their money out of the stock market if there is fear.   Example: if we go to War. It could be any major event. A perfect example is back in 2008 when people were defaulting on their mortgage loans. The stock market went so low, much lower than 9-11

The biggest obstacle is to hear the News as soon as possible. Most people are usually at work or they don't have real time information. You want to act fast because the population will all be doing the same.

If everyone wants to buy the stock share of a great company the price will go up. If everyone wants to sell the stock share the price goes down.

Here are some examples. Wayne hears the News at 8AM that the company Blue, stock went up 15% since the beginning of the year and he will buy the stock at $10 dollars a share. If Judy hears the News at 11AM she will buy the stock Blue at $13 a share. Judy pays more for one stock share. The market is climbing and the stock shares are getting more expensive.

Here is the opposite. If Lisa hears the News at 8AM that many states were hit by tornado. She will get nervous and sell her stock called yellow tail thinking this tornado will affect many people. So, she sells her stock at $20 a share and gets her money back. If Greg hears the News at 11AM he will want to sell his stock yellow tail. He receives $15 a share. The price of the yellow stock share keeps going down because no one wants the stock.

CHAPTER 4. STOCKS

When did stocks begin? It dates back to the 1792 and further back. The exchange traces its roots to the 1600's. A stock represents ownership in a company. People buy a stock because they think the company will do well over time. The stock share price will change over time. If many people are buying a company stock, the stock share price will go up. If people are selling a stock share the price will go down.

Companies will sell stocks within their company to raise money to fund operations. They can improve the current products they have, hire more employees and many other things

Many people are confused about the stock market. You see all these numbers, lines and charts. It is totally understandable. The majority of people will just listen to people they trust. Yup, heard it through the grapevine. Many people heard that song. It's the good old rumor.

Sadly, people do not even do research or know how to research. So, many people just invest and they are lost. Some never enter the stock market again.

This is a perfect example. Uncle Charlie Beach comes to a family function and he is bragging to his family his stock called Pink Piggy. He goes on saying he made 10% rate of return last year. Uncle Charlie Beach is rich, drives a Mercedes Benz and Lexus He also lives in an upscale apartment.

Michael T, Dean E, and Bernie F within Uncle Charlie Beach's family buy the Pink Piggy stock. For the first three months it is doing great. The fourth month the company

makes a public statement announcing they are closing some retail stores.
The stock share price goes down much lower than Bernie B, Michael T, and Dean E. purchased from the beginning.
Uncle Charlie Beach forgot to tell them about his other stocks that were down last year. He wanted everyone to think he knew the stock market better than everyone.

He did not tell them the golden rule: past performance is not necessarily indicative of future results. You will read that constantly with investments. It is a regulatory risk warning on investments material that everyone knows but not many people seem to actually implement into their decision making.

So, they all called Uncle Charlie Beach and he does not respond for two days, in the meantime the stock is sliding down. They all sell their stock in a panic and take a big loss. Uncle Charlie Beach returns their calls with sadness. He goes on to say I am just as sad. My landlord gave me one week to leave my apartment because I could not pay the rent for months.

So, what happen to Uncle Charlie? Oh, you didn't read? What would I know this was just an example. I thought that was funny.

My older cousin, Debbie would always talk about money. She had a lot of coin, very hardworking and frugal. She was very bright in school and went into the medical field.

I remember her saying the gold sector is doing great and I will continue to keep investing my money there. At that time, I was about 24 years old and I knew a decent amount about investments. I said nothing because I knew everything changes. No one would listen anyway.

A year later precious metals went down. Every time I saw her, I would joke with her. The information you will read many, times is when the stock market goes down, gold, silver, metals will rise. Although, with my personal experience it did not happen.

CHAPTER 5. CONSERVATIVE INVESTING

The most conservative way to invest in the stock market is to buy a mutual fund which hold many stocks. What is that called? A mutual fund or ETF (exchange trade fund.) The major difference is a mutual fund is closely managed. Investing in a mutual fund or ETF is a longer- term commitment.

There are so many to choose. How do you choose?
I mentioned before the S&P 500 which performs just like the over-all stock market is actually the oldest and most popular. There is the Dow 30 and Nasdaq which to me are risker.

There are some mutual funds and ETF's that are based on the age you will retire. If someone plans on retiring at 2030, the mutual fund or ETF will become safer towards 2030. They will move the money to cash or another guaranteed investment.

The reason why I mention conservative investing is people hear the News about a particular stock and by the time they hear the News the money wave is over.
Investing in mutual fund or ETF moves slow since there are many stocks within the investment.

It is very easy to find information on mutual funds and ETF's. You can easily research mutual funds or ETF'S all over the internet. You will find the risk factor, the companies in the fund they invest in. When it comes to money or any investment. If you are on the fence about anything you are thinking of investing in, make no decision. If you must decide on a decision then that is totally different.

When we read about investments you will see many charts referring to your age. Personally, I did not follow it and I do not follow it today. I believe people should do what they feel comfortable doing for their life. How can anyone plan their life so far ahead?

For example, if you are 42 years old you should have 50% in stocks in your financial portfolio. There is also the 60 40 Rule. For example, at any age you should have 60% in stocks and 40% in bonds. There is also many charts and graphs if you are this age or that age.

We earn our money and we want to shelter it. Everyone thinks different about money. I suppose that's why they say never mention the subject money in a conservation. If you are deciding anything about a financial move, make sure you are feeling well balance. Our emotions are so important to our actions.

If you are going through a major episode in your life, again make no decision. Your emotions could be very sad, with that step away. It is no time to make financial major decisions. It could even be very happy. If you back in your past you may know what I am mentioning here.

What about investing in one of those companies within the S&P 500. I do hold shares in McDonalds and other stocks. MCD stock has gone up over the years. The stock chart is very good from many years ago. MCD is what they call the ticker. I have no ideal other than it is a shorter name than McDonalds. I love McDonalds and my niece and I would go to just get the toy they were giving out.

Here is some room to write down notes. Research companies and see if you want to look at their past.

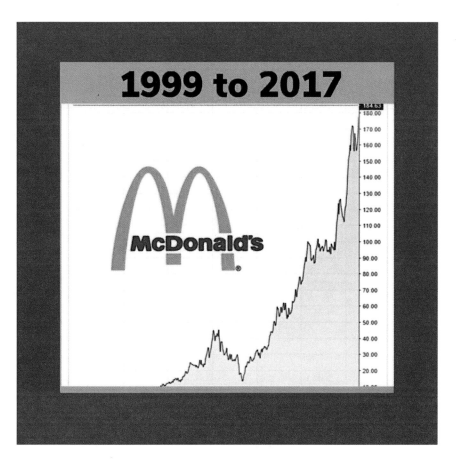

If you look further back in time you will view the same upscale chart. Many people will choose what item they follow or admire. McDonald's – I'm loving it.

That's their slogan.

CHAPTER 6 – DOLLAR COST AVERAGING

WHATTTTT? What is that? The first time I heard that I was thinking a dollar cost can be average? What is average if we think about just a dollar?

Buying at all different times with stock shares gives you a chance to get the best price overall.

Here is a perfect example:

Victor goes to Macy's in January and has $100 dollars. He buys one pair of jeans for $100 dollars.

Lisa is on a very limited budget. She has three kids and cannot think of spending that much on one pair of jeans for $100 dollars. She is a bargain shopper so her children can all have clothing.

She goes to Macy's in February and has $100 dollars. She buys the same pair of jeans for $50 dollars that Victor purchased. In March, she buys the same pair of jeans for $25 dollars. In May, she buys the same pair of jeans for $25 dollars.

Again, buying at all different times with stock market shares gives you a chance to get the best price overall.

CHAPTER 7 – THE TIME VALUE OF MONEY

Simple interest

If you took $100 hundred dollars and placed it in the bank. The bank gave you 8% that was calculated **annually (year).**
At the end of the year, you would have $8.00 so the total would be $108.00.

I suppose that is why they call it simple interest. To me it was confusing. Why not just call it interest and an example would be helpful to all. The bank provides all these names without examples.

So, if I go to the bank at any given year, you will receive **$8 dollars a year.** If I go to the bank after **2 years**, I will receive $8 a year which equals x 2 equals $16 dollars the total would be $116.

So here we go again! Compound interest? Really? Another term that confuses that public. Honestly, I do not think I ever used that word in one sentence. I remember   my grandma saying   compound. I didn't even know then what it was, other than her making cookies.

I think of compounding is piling one cookie over the next cookie to get a bigger cookie.

It is your money getting interest every day.

You always want to obtain **daily compound interest**. Stocks and fund offer daily compound interest which means more money in the long run. Just remember daily compound interest is the best.

To follow are examples how time effects investments. The time value of compound interest is truly amazing.

If you invest $100 dollars after 10 years the total is $222.53

If you invest $100 dollars after 30 years the total is $1102.03

Imagine if we started investing at 10 years old. You have to be 18 years old to invest in your own account. Although, parents can set up a custodial account.

If you are interested in more examples, just go to investor.org
It will show you the great difference if you invest with simpleor compound interest.
As I wrote before, the best way to make the most money is to have compound interest and the longer time you invest like 20, 30 years the more money.

CHAPTER 8 – MY PAINFUL EXPERIENCE

If you ever want to really talk to someone, just ask them about themselves. So many times, we want to go up to someone that we really would like to know. We can't think of one thing to say that make sense.

Maybe just ask them how do you get an A on that test. Then the conservation drags on. One hour later as you are looking at clock you wished you did not even ask. Well. they may even tell you exactly how and just take the knowledge and run. That sounds good to me.

It is important to know my experience because I had no direct guidance or mentor probably just like you. It was so confusing but I definitely had a desire to learn. Maybe I was brainwashed by my family. Most of us are a product of our environment. Well, that's is what they tell me.

Okay, I shared my knowledge of making money. I will guide you further. Having money makes your life 100% better. Although, I believe if you have love is more important. It would be great to have both.

Everyone has their story and here is mine:

I was the last child born out of 4, so that meant every hand-me-down was tossed to me. I tell you there is nothing like wearing clothes that are worn and sometimes stained. What did I know, I was just a child.

I grew up in Newark, New Jersey. It was the semi-ghetto where I was born. It was around the major historical riot in Newark, New Jersey. Mom is a retired house wife-domestic Engineer. Just having four children is enough to make any parent overworked.

In high school, my dad had an unbelieve wrestling record, no one would ever actually believe. He received a full scholarship to any college. After college he went into the military and switched to teaching. He taught mathematics and eventually was inducted to the Hall of Fame for wrestling.

Does anyone know what it is like having a parent in the military? My Dad was very tough on us. He had to be frugal as a teacher; he made very little money. He knew the price of everything counting every dime. I began to think, if I ever had the chance to make money, I will finally would be happier.

I was the shortest girl in the class and I had this habit of rocking my head right to left all the time and I did not have much of an appetite. The doctor said I was fine. This is just a habit that many people.

I still rock my head from right to left. I am a very slow driver mostly because I don't want to kill any animals. So, can you imagine seeing me on the road rocking my head right to left and driving? People are always speeding by but I just laugh.

During the Holidays, we went to my Uncle Teddy's and Aunts house.   My Uncle was the nicest and smartest in the family. He was a wealth of knowledge as he was an intellect.

I remember he would just sit at the holiday table and listen to our conversation and walk outside to smoke. Puff away. Something interesting when a really smart person does something human like smoke a cigarette or even use profanity. I always thought the real smart people did everything that was healthy like they were perfect.

The reality is most people inherit their genes from the past generation. If you are really smart, it just means there are more connecters in your brain. I am 4'8 my parents are vertically challenged.

I always thought he needed a break from all the chatter. I would look at him and thought he really was one in a million. He was for sure.

I would go down to my uncle's library. I remember smelling the leather couches and the hard wood floors. It was like a museum. There had to be 200 books. Many were medical books and the stock market books.

The one thing that was clear is when my Uncle Teddy spoke everyone shut up and listened. Why? He was happy and rich. The subject was always the stock market.

During one holiday, I had the confidence to ask my uncle: can I borrow one of these books? He said take anyone you want and keep it. I was so elated with his generosity.

Honestly, it was a book I could fully understand. I read this elementary book purchased my own and gave his back.

I am not a genius, but when it came to work, I worked. Heck, my father would come in my room on a Saturday raise the shades at 9AM and say get up. I was not allowed to go out on Sundays. He wanted me to be successful. Now, it would make more sense if he told me the training drill and what it was actually for. Right?

I was delivering newspapers when I was 12 years old for 3 long years. In the snow and hot heat at 6AM every day. It was the Star Ledger, heavy paper. My parents were against it. They were serious and concerned. I remember saying I am doing it.

I didn't even think twice who was sleeping in or who didn't work at my age. I just jumped on my bike every morning. I remember my hands were so chapped they would bleed.

In school, I was always the student that showed up to the class early and left after everyone else. Hey, my dad was a school teacher and frowned at a "C" grade. In grammar school, I was voted miss personality. In high school, I received a scholarship and received an outstanding award for foreign language.

When I started working full-time early on, I read several books on the stock market. I purchased my first three stocks. My neighbor, Greg would go back and forth about the stock market. We thought we were rich. We were living home with our parents...lol

My stocks were losing money after 6 months, so I sold all 3 stocks. I was devastated and I lost money.

Another year went by and I studied books, articles, and literature. I had my lounge chair at the beach listening to loud music I probably missed a few pages but I did feel successful.

Honestly, I looked around at all the guys playing volley ball and the gals reading their magazines. I remember thinking these are rich kids. In the back of my mind, I was a kid who grew up with less and wanted to make my dad proud. With about 5,000 thoughts it is a challenge to always be positive.

My dog, Taffy gave me the most love. All of my pets did the same. Such innocent souls. That is exactly why I founded a charity for the homeless cats and dogs. Okay, enough about me.

Chapter 9 – THE BULLS, THE BEARS AND THE PIGS?

The bulls make money, the bears make money and the pigs make nothing. These names are scary. It makes the public think this could never be easy to learn the stock market.

 Why couldn't it be the bunny, the kitten and the puppy.? I think many more people would want to learn the stock market. New people who are learning the stock market hear bull bear market and they are totally confused.

The bull stock market means the stock market is up. Bull markets last longer than bear markets.

The bear market means the stock market is down. The bears do make money but that's a risk. People who invert the stock market can make money. You do not need to know that nor do I promote it.

Overall, the market has gone up since 1900.   Why? Again, one of the reasons is more people in the world.

This clearly shows the bull is the winner. The stock market is up. When you see the pictures out there you will most likely see the bull on top of the bear. You will see many pictures and the bull is on top of the bear. We all want the bull to win. Just means the people want the stock market going up.

CHAPTER 10 – SILVER AND GOLD

Silver and gold silver and gold. Did you ever watch Rudolph the Red nose Reindeer? The Christmas cartoon show. Remember Cornelius always looking for silver and gold? Did he find any? Nope, zip, zero, nothing. So funny when he says tah tah nothing.

Well, it's not too funny with me. I bought a mutual fund about 15 years ago that mirrors silver and gold. I was thinking I had a lot of time why not. I swear as soon as I purchased it not bull was insight.

I always read the gold and silver precious metal sector in the stock market will go up when the overall stock market goes down. Really? Mine went south and south. Just goes to prove nothing is guaranteed in the stock market.

Thankfully, I did not put a lot of money into it. Imagine, I am still debating should I sell it. I waited this long so I guess I will keep it. I just laugh every time I see my Fidelity account.

Do you hear the commercials buy a chuck junk bullion of silver and gold? Advertising silver and gold will go up. How would they know? They do not. They are just trying to sell their product.

I swear it comes on every time I turn on the TV. You can't give a gold or silver bar bullion to the cashier at Shop Rite. You can't pull up to the gas station with your bullion and think you will get gas. The gas attendant will think you are clearly outside your mind. "Listen buddy take your car and get lost, look behind you I have 3 cars waiting for gas."

I am going to summarize this book. If you invest in the index S&P 500, there are 500 major companies in USA. Again, look at the chart since 1880. It is safer than one stock or several. Practice Dollar cost averaging and have a plan and back-up plan. As we know nothing is guaranteed so things change.

Okay, everyone time to go to the beach. Remember the sun tan lotion. Go golfing and shine up that club.

Thank you so much for reading.

There are so many people who think humans are far more important than any living being to the point where they will step on an ant, like it has no purpose in this life. It's not until all the humans let you down that you will seek something that you thought had no meaning.

KAREN JEAN ANTOINETTE D'ALESSANDRO

INDEX

Made in United States
North Haven, CT
15 May 2023

36594663R00020